TO
_____

FROM
_____

Words to Warm a Grandmother's Heart
© 2008 Summerside Press
www.summersidepress.com

Cover & Interior Design by
Müllerhaus Publishing Group | www.mullerhaus.net

Scripture references are from the following sources: The Holy Bible, New International Version® NIV®. © 1973, 1978, 1984 by International Bible Society. Used by permission of Zondervan. The New King James Version (NKJV). Copyright © 1982 by Thomas Nelson, Inc. Used by permission. The Holy Bible, New Living Translation® (NLT). Copyright © 1996, 2004. Used by permission of Tyndale House Publishers, Inc., Wheaton, Illinois. The Message © 1993, 1994, 1995, 1996, 2000, 2001, 2002 by Eugene Peterson. Used by permission of NavPress, Colorado Springs, CO. The New Century Version® (NCV). Copyright © 1987, 1988, 1991 by Thomas Nelson, Inc. Used by permission. All rights reserved.

Excluding Scripture verses, references to men and masculine pronouns have been replaced with gender-neutral references.

ISBN 978-1-934770-25-2

Printed in China

WORDS TO WARM
· · · A · · ·
Grandmother's
HEART

summerside
PRESS

TABLE OF CONTENTS

. . . .

Lifetime
Impressions

A grandmother can be one of the most important
teachers a child ever has.

The popular idea that a child forgets easily
is not an accurate one.
Many people go right through life
in the grip of an idea which has been impressed
on them in very tender years.

AGATHA CHRISTIE

What we feel, think, and do this moment
influences both our present and the future
in ways we may never know.
Begin. Start right where you are.
Consider your possibilities and find inspiration...
to add more meaning and zest to your life.

ALEXANDRA STODDARD

Trust in the Lord with all your heart, and lean not on your
own understanding; in all your ways acknowledge Him,
and He shall direct your paths.

PROVERBS 3:5-6 NKJV

* * * * * * * * * * * * * * * * * * *

There is no greater joy nor greater reward
than to make a fundamental difference in
someone's life.

MARY ROSE McGEADY

The blossom cannot tell what becomes of its fragrance as
it drifts away, just as no person can tell what becomes of
her influence as she continues through life.

The human contribution is the essential ingredient. It is
only in the giving of oneself to others that we truly live.

ETHEL PERCY ANDRUS

A hug delights and warms and charms.
It must be why God gave us arms.
And no one knows a hug as dear
As when we have our Grandma near.

Kindness is the only service that will stand the storm
of life and not wash out. It will wear well and be
remembered long after the prism of politeness or the
complexion of courtesy has faded away.

*We can't all be shining examples,
but we can at least twinkle a little.*

Train up a child in the way he should go,
and when he is old he will not depart from it.

PROVERBS 22:6 NKJV

The fullness of our heart is expressed in our eyes,
in our touch, in what we write, in what we say,
in the way we walk, the way we receive,
the way we need.

MOTHER TERESA

The real secret of happiness is not what you give
or what you receive, it's what you share.

A child's hand in yours—what tenderness
and power it arouses. You are instantly the very
touchstone of wisdom and strength.

MARJORIE HOLMES

There are two kinds of people in the world:
those who come into a room and say, "Here I am!"
and those who come in and say, "Ah, there you are!"

When we do the best that we can, we never know what
miracle is wrought in our life,
or in the life of another.

HELEN KELLER

This I learned from the shadow of a tree,
That to and fro did sway against a wall,
Our shadow selves, our influence, may fall
Where we ourselves can never be.

ANNA HAMILTON

Guide older women into lives of reverence so they
end up...models of goodness. By looking at them,
the younger women will know how to love their
husbands and children, be virtuous and pure.

TITUS 2:2-5 THE MESSAGE

Grandma, thank you for your kind heart and
laughing eyes, for warm cookies and hugs.
Most of all, Grandma, thank you for your constant
love and support.

Some people make the world special just by being in it.

I Have a Grateful Heart

If we learn how to give of ourselves,
to forgive others, and to live with thanksgiving,
we need not seek happiness.
It will seek us.

Feeling grateful or appreciative of someone or something in your life actually attracts more of the things that you appreciate and value into your life. And, the more of your life that you like and appreciate, the healthier you'll be.

CHRISTIANE NORTHRUP

A grandmother is all those wonderful things you never outgrow your need for.

God, of Your goodness give me Yourself, for You are enough for me. And only in You do I have everything.

JULIAN OF NORWICH

Let us come before His presence with thanksgiving; Let us shout joyfully to Him with psalms.

PSALM 95:2 NKJV

To receive a gift, molded from love and sacrifice,
selected with care and tied up with all the excitement
the giver has to offer, is indeed rare.
They don't come along often,
but when they do, cherish them.

ERMA BOMBECK

The neatest thing about our Granny
is that every one of us was her favorite.

Gratitude unlocks the fullness of life. It turns what we
have into enough, and more.... It can turn a meal into
a feast, a house into a home, a stranger into a friend.
Gratitude makes sense of our past, brings peace for today,
and creates a vision for tomorrow.

MELODY BEATTIE

Give thanks to God. Call out His name.
Ask Him anything! Shout to the nations, tell them what
He's done, spread the news of His great reputation!

ISAIAH 12:4 THE MESSAGE

Friendships, family ties, the companionship
of little children, an autumn forest flung in prodigality
against a deep blue sky, the intricate design and haunting
fragrance of a flower, the counterpoint of a Bach fugue or
the melodic line of a Beethoven sonata,
the fluted note of bird song,
the glowing glory of a sunset:
the world is aflame with things of eternal moment.

E. MARGARET CLARKSON

That I am here is a wonderful mystery to which
I will respond with joy.

Most of the people I know who have what
I want—which is to say, purpose, heart, balance,
gratitude, joy—are people with a deep sense of
spirituality…. They are part of something beautiful.

ANNE LAMOTT

Peace is seeing a sunset and knowing who to thank.

The day is done, the sun has set,
Yet light still tints the sky;
My heart stands still
In reverence,
For God is passing by.

RUTH ALLA WAGER

Let the peace of Christ rule in your hearts, since as
members of one body you were called to peace.
And be thankful. Let the word of Christ dwell in you
richly as you teach and admonish one another with all
wisdom, and as you sing psalms, hymns and
spiritual songs with gratitude in your hearts to God.

COLOSSIANS 3:15-16 NIV

Happiness is a healthy mental attitude, a grateful spirit,
a clear heart full of love.

Were there no God we would be in this glorious world
with grateful hearts and no one to thank.

CHRISTINA ROSSETTI

I love Grandma because she gives the biggest and
the best hugs. I feel happy when she holds me.

The wonder of living is held
within the beauty of silence,
the glory of sunlight...
the sweetness of fresh spring air,
the quiet strength of earth,
and the love that lies
at the very root of all things.

Discovering Joy

Children help us rediscover the joy, excitement, and mystery of the world we live in.

Grandma,
Thoughts of you bring thoughts of joy…
Because you have touched my life
With the love of the Lord.

If one is joyful, it means that one is faithfully
living for God, and that nothing else counts; and if
one gives joy to others one is doing God's work.
With joy without and joy within,
all is well.

JANET ERSKINE STUART

Grandmas don't just say "that's nice"—they reel back
and roll their eyes and throw up their hands and smile.
You get your money's worth out of grandmas.

I pray that the God who gives hope will fill you with much
joy and peace while you trust in Him. Then your hope will
overflow by the power of the Holy Spirit.

ROMANS 15:13 NCV

*May happiness touch your life today
as warmly as you have touched
the lives of others.*

At the sound of a child's pure laugh or
the sight of a father holding his baby for the first time,
incredible joy pushes upward, spilling over.
Our hearts were made for joy. Our hearts were made to
enjoy the One who created them. Too deeply planted to be
much affected by the ups and downs of life,
this joy is a knowing and a being known by our Creator.
He sets our hearts alight with radiant joy.

I've grown to realize the joy that comes from little
victories is preferable to the fun that comes from ease
and the pursuit of pleasure.

LAWANA BLACKWELL

To be able to find joy in another's joy,
that is the secret of happiness.

How necessary it is to cultivate a spirit of joy.
It is a psychological truth that the physical acts of
reverence and devotion make one feel devout.
The courteous gesture increases one's respect for others.
To act lovingly is to begin to feel loving,
and certainly to act joyfully brings joy to others
which in turn makes one feel joyful.
I believe we are called to the duty of delight.

DOROTHY DAY

Favorite people, favorite places,
favorite memories of the past...
These are the joys of a lifetime...
these are the things that last.

Now that I've reached the age, or maybe the stage,
where I need my children more than they need me,
I really understand how grand it is to be a grandmother.

MARGARET WHITLAM

All who seek the Lord will praise Him.
Their hearts will rejoice with everlasting joy.

PSALM 22:26 NLT

*If we celebrate the years behind us they
become stepping-stones of strength and joy
for the years ahead.*

When hands reach out in friendship,
hearts are touched with joy.

As we grow in our capacities to see and enjoy
the joys that God has placed in our lives,
life becomes a glorious experience of discovering
His endless wonders.

You will show me the path of life;
in Your presence is fullness of joy;
at Your right hand are pleasures forevermore.

PSALM 16:11 NKJV

Happiness is like a butterfly. The more you chase it,
the more it will elude you.
But if you turn your attention to other things,
it comes and softly sits on your shoulder.

God
Our Father

Be still, and in the quiet moments, listen to the voice of
your heavenly Father. His words can renew your spirit...
no one knows you and your needs like He does.

Janet Weaver Smith

God will never let you be shaken or
moved from your place near His heart.

JONI EARECKSON TADA

The Creator thinks enough of you to have
sent Someone very special so that you might
have life—abundantly, joyfully,
completely, and victoriously.

How great is the love the Father
has lavished on us,
that we should be called children of God!
And that is what we are!

1 JOHN 3:1 NIV

God is every moment totally aware of each one of us.
Totally aware in intense concentration and love....
No one passes through any area of life, happy or tragic,
without the attention of God.

EUGENIA PRICE

My grandma likes to play with God,
They have a kind of game.
She plants the garden full of seeds,
He sends the sun and rain.
She likes to sit and talk with God
And knows He is right there.
She prays about the whole wide world,
Then leaves us in His care.

ANN JOHNSON, AGE 8

Whoever walks toward God one step,
God runs toward him two.

JEWISH PROVERB

People who don't know God
and the way He works
fuss over these things,
but you know both God
and how He works.
Steep yourself in God-reality,
God-initiative, God-provisions.
You'll find all your everyday
human concerns will be met.
Don't be afraid of missing out.
You're My dearest friends!
The Father wants to give you
the very kingdom itself.

LUKE 12:30-32 THE MESSAGE

Stand outside this evening. Look at the stars.
Know that you are special and loved by
the One who created them.

Perhaps this moment is unclear, but let it be—even if
the next, and many moments after that are unclear,
let them be. Trust that God will help you work them out,
and that all the unclear moments will bring you to
that moment of clarity and action when you are known
by Him and know Him. These are the
better and brighter moments of His blessing.

*As a rose fills a room with its fragrance,
so will God's love will our lives.*

MARGARET BROWNLEY

Grace and peace to you from God our Father
and the Lord Jesus Christ.

ROMANS 1:7 NCV

The God who created, names, and numbers the stars in
the heavens also numbers the hairs of my head....
He pays attention to very big things
and to very small ones.
What matters to me matters to Him,
and that changes my life.

ELISABETH ELLIOT

Before anything else, above all else,
beyond everything else, God loves us. God loves us
extravagantly, ridiculously, without limit or condition.
God is in love with us...God yearns for us.

ROBERTA BONDI

It is only a tiny rosebud—
A flower of God's design;
But I cannot unfold the petals
With these clumsy hands of mine.
For the pathway that lies before me
My Heavenly Father knows—
I'll trust Him to unfold the moments
Just as He unfolds the rose.

She
Who Laughs

It's funny—just plain funny—to see your own baby
with a baby of her own.

Mrs. Clipston Sturgis

If becoming a grandmother was only a matter of choice
I should advise every one of you straight away
to become one. There is no fun for old people like it!

HANNAH WHITALL SMITH

*Our mouths were filled with laughter,
our tongues with songs of joy.*

PSALM 126:2 NIV

Today's Forecast: Partly rational with brief periods
of coherent thought giving way to complete
apathy by tonight.

SHERRIE WEAVER

Take time to laugh. It is the music of the soul.

People can be divided into three groups:
Those who make things happen,
those who watch things happen,
and those who wonder what happened.

The best laughter, the laughter that can heal,
the laughter that has the truest ring, is the laughter that
flowers out of a love for life and its Giver.

MAXINE HANCOCK

The trouble with being an optimist is that people think
you don't know what's going on.

Laugh at yourself first before anyone else can.

ELSA MAXWELL

Sense of humor; God's great gift
causes spirits to uplift,
Helps to make our bodies mend;
lightens burdens; cheers a friend;
Tickles children; elders grin
at this warmth that glows within;
Surely in the great hereafter
heaven must be full of laughter!
A cheerful heart is good medicine.

PROVERBS 17:22 NIV

If you can learn to laugh in spite of the circumstances
that surround you, you will enrich others, enrich yourself,
and more than that, you will last!

BARBARA JOHNSON

Blessed are they who can laugh at themselves,
for they shall never cease to be amused.

Give me a sense of humor, Lord,
Give me the grace to see a joke,
To get some happiness from life
And pass it on to other folk.

*A good laugh is as good
as a prayer sometimes.*

LUCY MAUD MONTGOMERY

Most of the time my Granny had a grin.
It was the look of joy; the look of delight;
and it also contained a little mischief in it,
the spirit of fun.

In the world you will have tribulation;
but be of good cheer, I have overcome the world.

JOHN 16:33 NKJV

Grandmas know the value of lumpiness in
Christmas packaging.

JUDITH C. GRANT

Whole-hearted, ready laughter heals, encourages,
relaxes anyone within hearing distance.
The laughter that springs from love
makes wide the space around—
gives room for the loved one to enter in.

EUGENIA PRICE

I am fully aware that my youth has been spent,
that my get up and go has got up and went.
But I really don't mind, when I think with a grin,
of all the grand places my get up has been.

The Gifts We're Given

Grandma,
God has gifted you
In uniquely beautiful ways
To bless the lives of others.
You are special!

I love to open my door
and see my Granny standing there.
It's like opening up a gift from God.

GRACIE FAULKENBERRY, AGE 5

There is no better gift I can give my grandchildren than
to show them how to keep a quiet heart in this
loud and busy world.

We should make the most of what God gives,
both the bounty and the capacity to enjoy it,
accepting what's given and delighting in the work.
It's God's gift! God deals out joy in the present, the now.

ECCLESIASTES 5:18 THE MESSAGE

God gave me my gifts.
I will do all I can to show Him
how grateful I am to Him.

GRACE LIVINGSTON HILL

This is the real gift: you have been given
the breath of life, designed with a unique,
one-of-a-kind soul that exists forever—
the way that you choose to live it
doesn't change the fact that you've been
given the gift of being now and forever.
Priceless in value, you are handcrafted by God,
who has a personal design and plan for each of us.

It is clear to us, friends, that God not only loves you
very much but also has put His hand on you
for something special.

1 THESSALONIANS 1:4 THE MESSAGE

Let us examine our capacities and gifts,
and then put them to the best use we may.
As our own view of life is of necessity partial,
I do not find that we can do better than to put them
absolutely in God's hands, and look to Him
for the direction of our lives....
God can do great things with our lives,
if we but give them to Him in sincerity.

ANNA R. B. LINDSAY

Since you are like no other being ever created since
the beginning of time, you are incomparable.

BRENDA UELAND

When I stand before God at the end of my life,
I would hope that I would not have a single bit of talent
left and could say, "I used everything You gave me."

ERMA BOMBECK

Because He was full of grace and truth,
from Him we all received one gift after another.

JOHN 1:16 NCV

*Lord, give me the special gift of being able to
view the world through the eyes of a child.*

Each one of us is God's special work of art.
Through us, He teaches and inspires,
delights and encourages, informs and
uplifts all those who view our lives.

JONI EARECKSON TADA

God does not ask your ability or your inability.
He asks only your availability.

MARY KAY ASH

God gave us Grandmothers
because He knew,
there are some things
only Grandmas can do.
Stories just she knows
that need to be told
Hugs that get born
in a heart made of gold.
God sends us so many
things from above,
Delivered by Grandmothers
wrapped up in love.

God's designs regarding you, and His methods
of bringing about these designs, are infinitely wise.

MADAME JEANNE GUYON

Love
All Around

We see those we love
in every sunrise and in every sunset,
in every tree and in every flower.

My Granny's house was like a second home to me.
I could go there anytime and find her door open,
ready to receive me, her smile warm and inviting,
and her arms stretched out in love.

Open your hearts to the love God instills....
God loves you tenderly. What He gives you
is not to be kept under lock and key,
but to be shared.

MOTHER TERESA

*Love, like sunshine's warmth, beams forth on
every side and bends to every need.*

Love...bears all things, believes all things,
hopes all things, endures all things. Love never fails.

1 CORINTHIANS 13:4, 7-8 NKJV

There is no need to plead that the love of God shall fill
our hearts as though He were unwilling to fill us....
Love is pressing around us on all sides like air.
Cease to resist it and instantly love takes possession.

AMY CARMICHAEL

What we have once enjoyed we can never lose.
All that we love deeply becomes a part of us.

HELEN KELLER

Grandma,
Your perseverance is an example of His faithfulness…
Your kindness a testimony of His mercy…
Your hope a witness to His sovereignty…
Your commitment a picture of His love.

Let's practice real love.
This is the only way
we'll know we're living truly,
living in God's reality.
It's also the way to shut down
debilitating self-criticism.... For God
is greater than our worried hearts
and knows more about us
than we do ourselves.
And friends, once that's taken care of
and we're no longer accusing
or condemning ourselves,
we're bold and free before God!

1 JOHN 3:18-21 THE MESSAGE

Nothing can separate you from His love,
absolutely nothing.... God is enough for time,
and God is enough for eternity.
God is enough!

HANNAH WHITALL SMITH

Only He who created the wonders of the world
entwines hearts in an eternal way.

In the effort to give good and comforting answers
to the young questioners whom we love,
we very often arrive at good and comforting
answers for ourselves.

RUTH GOODE

*Love…it begins with a moment that grows
richer and brighter…and becomes a
lifetime of joy.*

You shall love the Lord your God with all your heart,
with all your soul, and with all your strength.

DEUTERONOMY 6:5 NKJV

Lord, let the glow of Your love
Through my whole being shine.
Fill me with gladness from above
and hold me by strength Divine.
Lord, make Your Light in my Heart
Glow radiant and clear, never to part.

MARGARET FISHBACK POWERS

Your house is warm and safe, a place where children
want to come—where they can find a cool glass
of milk and fresh cookies, open arms
and a grandma's heart full of love.

A Friend in You

Someone to talk to, to laugh with, to tell secrets to....
Grandma, I'm just so thankful for the friend
I've found in you.

If we would build on a sure foundation in friendship,
we must love friends for their sake
rather than for our own.

CHARLOTTE BRONTË

Friends come and friends go,
but a true friend sticks by you like family.

PROVERBS 18:24 THE MESSAGE

The happiest business in all the world
is that of making friends,
And no investment on the street
pays larger dividends,
For life is more than stocks and bonds,
and love than rate percent,
And she who gives in friendship's name
shall reap what she has spent.

Insomuch as any one pushes you nearer to God,
he or she is your friend.
FRENCH PROVERB

The closest friends I have made all through life
have been people who also grew up close
to a loved and loving grandmother.
MARGARET MEAD

Don't walk in front of me—I may not follow.
Don't walk behind me—I may not lead.
Walk beside me—And just be my friend.

There is nothing better than the
encouragement of a good friend.

KATHARINE BUTLER HATHAWAY

I am only as strong as the coffee I drink,
the hairspray I use, and the friends I have.

Stay true to the Lord. I love you and long to see you,
dear friends, for you are my joy.

PHILIPPIANS 4:1 NLT

When things aren't going well, I can always count on Grandma. She comes out and brightens up the day just like the sun.

Having someone who understands is a great blessing
for ourselves. Being someone who understands
is a great blessing to others.

JANETTE OKE

Grandparents are pretty special,
they are friends of treasured worth...
and one who knows their love
has the greatest gift on earth.

Friendship is the fruit gathered from the trees
planted in the rich soil of love, and nurtured with
tender care and understanding.

ALMA L. WEIXELBAUM

A friend hears the song in my heart
and sings it to me when my memory fails.

The comfort of knowing that our bond will survive
despite our differences and that our connection provides
each of us with a more accurate picture of ourselves
enhances our chances of finding inner peace and
satisfaction as we age together.

JANE MERSKY LEDER

This is My commandment, that you love one other
as I have loved you. Greater love has no one than this,
than to lay down one's life for his friends.

JOHN 15:12-13 NKJV

A friend understands what you are trying to say...
even when your thoughts aren't fitting into words.

ANN D. PARRISH

Knowing what to say is not always necessary;
just the presence of a caring friend can make
a world of difference.

SHERI CURRY

Beautiful and rich is an old friendship
Grateful to the touch as ancient ivory,
Smooth as aged wine,
or sheen of tapestry
Where light has lingered,
intimate and long.

EUNICE TIETJENS

Grandma,
I keep so many treasures of our times together
and I hold you close in my heart.

Praise and Thanksgiving

Grandma, I'd like to pick a thousand wildflowers
and lay them at your feet, each one representing a prayer
of thankfulness to God for the gift of beauty
and joy you are in my life.

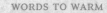

Grandmother was sitting in a low rocking-chair,
with the baby in her arms,
bending over it with eyes of worship.

LAURA E. RICHARDS

*Enter His gates with thanksgiving
and His courts with praise;
give thanks to Him and praise His name.*

PSALM 100:4 NIV

May your life become one of glad and unending praise
to the Lord as you journey through this world,
and in the world that is to come!

TERESA OF AVILA

Our thanksgiving today should include those
things which we take for granted, and we
should continually praise our God,
who is true to His promise, who has provided
and retained the necessities for our living.

BETTY FUHRMAN

They that trust the Lord find many things
to praise Him for. Praise follows trust.

LILY MAY GOULD

For childhood's golden memories
For happy bygone years
The comfort of your presence
In days of joy or tears
For all your love upon life's way—
I thank you from my heart this day.

I praise the Lord because He does what is right,
I sing praises to the Lord most high.

PSALM 7:17 NCV

Morning has broken like the first morning,
Blackbird has spoken like the first bird....
Praise with elation, praise every morning,
God's re-creation of the new day!

ELEANOR FARJEON

Although it be good to think upon
the kindness of God, and to love Him and
praise Him for it; yet it is far better to
gaze upon the pure essence of Him and
to love Him and praise Him for Himself.

*Thanksgiving puts power in living,
because it opens the generators of the heart
to respond gratefully, to receive joyfully,
and to react creatively.*

Let's praise His name! He is holy, He is almighty.
He is love. He brings hope, forgiveness, heart cleansing,
peace and power. He is our deliverer and coming King.
Praise His wonderful name!

LUCILLE M. LAW

We are Your people, the sheep of Your flock.
We will thank You always;
forever and ever we will praise You.

PSALM 79:13 NCV

Grandma,
For all of the memories of yesterday,
For the treasured gift of today,
For all we will share in the future…
Thank you.

Woven in a perfect way, a blanket of stars
covers the night sky, each star set in its place,
reflecting its perfect light.
All the stars together make a grand display,
glimmering and shimmering in a unique expression
of praise to the Creator of them all.

Let us give all that lies within us…to pure praise,
to pure loving adoration, and to worship
from a grateful heart—
a heart that is trained to look up.

AMY CARMICHAEL

The Heart of the Family

From the heart of a godly grandmother,
Living water flows…
Refreshing the lives of her family.

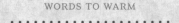

What families have in common the world around is that
they are the place where people learn who they are
and how to be that way.

JEAN ILLSLEY CLARKE

Please, bless my family.
Let it continue before You always.
Lord God, You have said so.

2 SAMUEL 7:29 NCV

We were a strange little band of characters,
trudging through life sharing diseases and toothpaste,
coveting one another's desserts, hiding shampoo,
borrowing money, locking each other out of our rooms,
inflicting pain and kissing to heal it in the same instant,
loving, laughing, defending, and trying to figure out
the common thread that bound us all together.

ERMA BOMBECK

Grandchildren are the dots that connect the lines from generation to generation.

LOIS WYSE

Family faces are magic mirrors. Looking at people who belong to us, we see the past, present, and future.

GAIL LUMET BUCKLEY

All of you should be in agreement,
understanding each other, loving each other as family,
being kind and humble.

1 PETER 3:8 NCV

There is nothing quite so deeply satisfying as the solidarity of a family united across the generations and miles by a common faith and history.

SARA WENGER SHENK

Call it clan, call it a network, call it a tribe, call it a family.
Whatever you call it, whoever you are, you need one.

Jane Howard

Follow the children. Hear the joy in their laughter.
See the love in their eyes. Feel the hope in their touch.

*There's no place like home—
except Grandma's.*

Sooner or later we all discover that the important
moments in life are not the advertised ones,
not the birthdays, the graduations, the weddings,
not the great goals achieved.
The real milestones are less prepossessing.
They come to the door of memory.

Susan B. Anthony

Families give us many things—love and meaning,
purpose and an opportunity to give,
and a sense of humor.

Childhood's days pass all too quickly,
Happy memories all too few;
Plan to do that special something,
Take the time to go or do.
Make a memory with your children,
Take the time in busy days;
Have some fun while they are growing,
Show your love in gentle ways.

ELAINE HARDT

The ultimate economic and spiritual unit
of any civilization is still the family.

CLARE BOOTH LUCE

We really need only five things on this earth: Some food,
some sun, some work, some fun, and someone.

BEATRICE NOLAN

You are citizens along with all of God's holy people.
You are members of God's family.

EPHESIANS 2:19 NLT

It takes a lifetime to get back to knowing
you don't know anything: that's why grandmothers
and grandchildren get on so well together.

The effect of having other interests
beyond those domestic works well.
The more one does and sees and feels,
the more one is able to do, and the more genuine
may be one's appreciation of fundamental things
like home, and love, and understanding companionship.

AMELIA EARHART

Grandmas should write down the stories of their lives,
however dull they seem to them. For such tales show
history as it is—a procession of interlocking lives.
A unity. The family of mankind.

CHARLOTTE GRAY

Priceless Prayer

There's no way to measure the value of a praying Grandmother. Prayer is one of the richest gifts a grandchild can receive.

If it is God who gives prayer,
then God often gives it in the form of gratitude,
and gratitude itself, when it is received attentively
in prayer, is healing to the heart.
Prayer is such a mysterious business
for something so ordinary and everyday.

ROBERTA BONDI

When we call on God, He bends down
His ear to listen, as a father bends down to
listen to his little child.

ELIZABETH CHARLES

If a care is too small to be turned into a prayer
then it is too small to be made into a burden.

When you were small
And just a touch away,
I covered you with blankets
Against the cool night air.
But now that you are tall
And out of reach,
I fold my hands
And cover you with prayer.

DONA MADDUX COOPER

Always be joyful. Pray continually, and give thanks
whatever happens. That is what God wants
for you in Christ Jesus.

1 THESSALONIANS 5:16-18 NCV

It is when things go wrong, when good things
do not happen, when our prayers seem
to have been lost,
that God is most present.

MADELEINE L'ENGLE

Sometimes, usually when I need it most,
I can feel my Granny's prayers.

We need quiet time to examine our lives openly
and honestly...spending quiet time alone
gives your mind an opportunity to
renew itself and create order.

SUSAN L. TAYLOR

We must take our troubles to the Lord,
but we must do more than that;
we must leave them there.

HANNAH WHITALL SMITH

I pray for a child-like heart,
For gentle, holy love,
For strength to do Thy will below,
As angels do above.

Allow your dreams a place in your prayers and plans.
God-given dreams can help you move into the future
He is preparing for you.

BARBARA JOHNSON

You are helping us by praying for us.
Then many people will give thanks because God
has graciously answered so many prayers

2 CORINTHIANS 1:11 NLT

The sunshine dancing on the water,
the lulling sound of waves rolling into the shore,
the glittering stars against the night sky—
all God's light, His warmth, His majesty—
our Father of light reaching out to us,
drawing each of us closer to Himself.

Open wide the windows of our spirits
and fill us full of light;
open wide the door of our hearts
that we may receive and
entertain Thee with all the powers
of our adoration.

CHRISTINA ROSSETTI

Pour out your heart to God your Father.
He understands you better than you do.

I thank my God every time I remember you,
always praying with joy for all of you.

PHILIPPIANS 1:3-4 NCV

You pay God a compliment by asking great things of Him.

TERESA OF AVILA

The Light of Faith

You are a child of your heavenly Father.
Confide in Him. Your faith in His love and power
can never be bold enough.

BASILEA SCHLINK

I learned a lot about the faithfulness of God
from my grandmother. I know I was never far
from her thoughts. She showed that in a thousand ways…
letters written to me at school, phone calls, little gifts
purchased here and there with me in mind.
She delighted in caring for me
not because of anything I did,
but simply because I was hers.

Faith sees the invisible,
believes the incredible,
and receives the impossible.

The Lord your God is indeed God.
He is the faithful God who keeps His covenant
for a thousand generations and lavishes
His unfailing love on those who love Him
and obey His commands.

DEUTERONOMY 7:9 NLT

I think miracles exist in part as gifts
and in part as clues that there is something
beyond the flat world we see.

PEGGY NOONAN

Faith expects from God
what is beyond all expectations.

The soft, sweet summer was warm and glowing,
Bright were the blossoms on every bough:
I trusted Him when the roses were blooming;
I trust Him now....

L. B. COWMAN

I pray that Christ will live in your hearts by faith
and that your life will be strong in love
and be built on love.

EPHESIANS 3:17 NCV

Faith means being sure of what we hope for...now.
It means knowing something is real, this moment,
all around you, even when you don't see it.
Great faith isn't the ability to believe long and far
into the misty future.
It's simply taking God at His word
and taking the next step.

JONI EARECKSON TADA

I believe in the sun even if it isn't shining.
I believe in love even when I am alone.
I believe in God even when He is silent.

Faithful, anointed one,
Vessel set apart as holy to the Lord;
Beacon of light in our family,
Servant of God.
My Grandmother, whom I love…
I honor you in the name of Jesus.

Ever since I first heard of your strong faith
in the Lord Jesus and your love
for God's people everywhere,
I have not stopped thanking God for you.
I pray for you constantly.

EPHESIANS 1:15-16 NLT

Within each of us
there is an inner place
where the living God Himself
longs to dwell,
our sacred center of belief.

I see Heaven's glories shine,
And faith shines equal, arming me from fear.

EMILY BRONTË

My prayer for you, Grandma, is that God's
faithfulness will encourage you today,
and that every moment will be filled
with reminders of His love.

Lord, thank You for my children.
Please inspire me with ways
to show them my love and Yours.
I want them to feel appreciated.
I want to help and encourage them....
I want to bless them.

QUIN SHERRER

Faith is not an effort, a striving, a ceaseless seeking,
as so many earnest souls suppose,
but rather a letting go, an abandonment,
an abiding rest in God that nothing,
not even the soul's shortcomings,
can disturb.

Setting Priorities

To be in your children's memories tomorrow,
you have to be in their lives today.

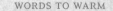
I hope my children look back on today,
And see a grandma who had time to play.
There will be years for cleaning and cooking,
For children grow up while we're not looking.

Let's not get tired of doing what is good....
Therefore, whenever we have the opportunity,
we should do good to everyone.

GALATIANS 6:9-10 NLT

Don't ever let yourself get so busy that you miss
those little but important extras in life—
the beauty of a day…the smile of a friend…
the serenity of a quiet moment alone.
For it is often life's smallest pleasures and gentlest joys
that make the biggest and most lasting difference.

Choices can change our lives profoundly.
The choice to mend a broken relationship,
to say yes to a difficult assignment,
to lay aside some important work to play with a child,
to visit some forgotten person—
these small choices may affect our lives eternally.

GLORIA GAITHER

*It is not how many years we live,
but what we do with them.*

CATHERINE BOOTH

Getting things accomplished isn't nearly as important
as taking time for love.

JANETTE OKE

We must not, in trying to think
about how we can make a big difference,
ignore the small daily differences we can
make which, over time, add up to
big differences that we often cannot foresee.

MARIAN WRIGHT EDELMAN

*Affection is the most satisfying reward a
child can receive. It costs nothing, is readily
available, and provides great encouragement.*

Becoming a grandparent is a second chance. For you
have a chance to put to use all the things you learned
the first time around and may have made a mistake on.
It's all love and no discipline.

JOYCE BROTHERS

If you look for Me wholeheartedly,
you will find Me.

JEREMIAH 29:13 NLT

• •

See each morning a world made anew,
as if it were the morning of the very first day;...
treasure and use it, as if it were the final hour
of the very last day.

FAY HARTZELL ARNOLD

Live for today but hold your hands open to tomorrow.
Anticipate the future and its changes with joy.
There is a seed of God's love in every event,
every circumstance, every unpleasant situation
in which you may find yourself.

BARBARA JOHNSON

Live each day the fullest you can,
not guaranteeing there'll be a tomorrow,
not dwelling endlessly on yesterday.

JANE SEYMOUR

Time is a very precious gift of God;
so precious that it's only given to us
moment by moment.

AMELIA BARR

Forgetting those things which are behind
and reaching forward to those things which are
ahead, I press toward the goal for the prize
of the upward call of God in Christ Jesus.

PHILIPPIANS 3:13-14 NKJV

Blessed is the person who is too busy to worry
in the daytime and too sleepy to worry at night.

CAROLINE SCHROEDER

Make the least of all that goes
and the most of all that comes.
Don't regret what is past.
Cherish what you have.
Look forward to all that is to come.
And most important of all,
rely moment by moment on Jesus Christ.

GIGI GRAHAM TCHIVIDJIAN

Words of Encouragement

Kids are like sponges:
They absorb all your strength and leave you limp.
But give 'em a squeeze and you get it all back.

There is nothing an old woman likes better
than to pick up the phone on a dull, dull day
and hear the clear, high voice of a grandchild
bursting with news.

PAM BROWN

You can get a lot of extra mileage
out of a grandmother
if you let her have a cup of tea.

CHARLOTTE GRAY

They have been a wonderful encouragement to me,
as they have been to you. You must show
your appreciation to all who serve so well.

1 CORINTHIANS 16:18 NLT

· ·

A word of encouragement to those we meet,
a cheerful smile in the supermarket, a card
or letter to a friend, a readiness to witness
when opportunity is given—
all are practical ways in which we may
let His light shine through us.

ELIZABETH B. JONES

The Scriptures give us hope and encouragement
as we wait patiently for God's promises to be fulfilled.

ROMANS 15:4 NLT

So many things we love are you...
flowers and beautiful handmade things—
small stitches.
So much of our reading and thinking,
so many sweet customs.... It is all you...
dear Grandma.

ANNE MORROW LINDBERGH

Some days, it is enough encouragement
just to watch the clouds break up
and disappear,
leaving behind a blue patch of sky
and bright sunshine
that is so warm upon my face.
It's a glimpse of divinity;
a kiss from heaven.

The stars exist that we might know
how high our dreams can soar.

If we help our children to be what they should be today,
then, when tomorrow becomes today,
they will have the necessary courage
to face it with greater love.

MOTHER TERESA

I'm sure now I'll see God's goodness
in the exuberant earth.
Stay with God! Take heart. Don't quit.

PSALM 27:13 THE MESSAGE

I wanted you to see what real courage is....
It's when you know you're licked before
you begin but you begin anyway
and you see it through no matter what.

HARPER LEE

Lord, make my life a living tribute
to the Godly example
of my grandmother.

There are times when encouragement means such a lot.
And a word is enough to convey it.

GRACE STRICKER DAWSON

Hope begins in the dark,
the stubborn hope that if you just show up
and try to do the right thing, the dawn will come.
You wait and watch and work: You don't give up.

ANNE LAMOTT

God is the sunshine that warms us,
the rain that melts the frost and waters the
young plants. The presence of God is a climate
of strong and bracing love, always there.

JOAN ARNOLD

Calm me, O Lord, as You stilled the storm,
Still me, O Lord, keep me from harm.
Let all the tumult within me cease,
Enfold me, Lord, in Your peace.

CELTIC TRADITIONAL

To Be
Content

An unhurried sense of time is
in itself a form of wealth.

BONNIE FRIEDMAN

May your footsteps set you upon a lifetime journey
of love. May you wake each day with God's blessings
and sleep each night in His keeping. And as you grow
older, may you always walk in His tender care.

Life is not intended to be simply a round of work,
no matter how interesting and important
that work may be. A moment's pause to watch
the glory of a sunrise or a sunset is soul satisfying,
while a bird's song will set the steps to music all day long.

LAURA INGALLS WILDER

Normal day, let me be aware of the treasure you are.
Let me learn from you, love you, bless you before
you depart. Let me not pass you by in quest
of some rare and perfect tomorrow.

We brought nothing into the world,
so we can take nothing out.
But, if we have food and clothes,
we will be satisfied with that.

I TIMOTHY 6:7-8 NCV

*Our fulfillment comes
in knowing God's glory,
loving Him for it,
and delighting in it.*

Oh, time! be slow! it was a dawn ago I was a child
dreaming of being grown; a noon ago I was with
children of my own; and now it's afternoon—
and late—and they are grown and gone. Time, wait!

RUTH BELL GRAHAM

I am still determined to be cheerful and happy,
in whatever situation I may be;
for I have also learned from experience
that the greater part of our happiness or misery
depends upon our dispositions,
and not upon our circumstances.

MARTHA WASHINGTON

Where the soul is full of peace and joy,
outward surroundings and circumstances
are of comparatively little account.

HANNAH WHITALL SMITH

A strong positive mental attitude will create
more miracles than any wonder drug.

PATRICIA NEAL

Let the day suffice, with all its joys and failings,
its little triumphs and defeats. I'd happily,
if sleepily, welcome evening as a time of rest,
and let it slip away, losing nothing.

KATHLEEN NORRIS

You're blessed when you're content
with just who you are—no more, no less.
That's the moment you find yourselves
proud owners of everything
that can't be bought.

MATTHEW 5:5 THE MESSAGE

A grandmother has ears that truly listen
and arms that always hold.
She has a love that's never-ending
and a heart made of purest gold.

It is always wise to stop wishing for things
long enough to enjoy the fragrance
of those now flowering.

PATRICE GIFFORD

Day-to-day living becomes a window through
which we get a glimpse of life eternal.
The eternal illuminates and gives focus to the daily.

JANICE RIGGLE HUIE

Contentment is not the fulfillment of what you want,
but the realization of how much you already have.

Godliness with contentment is great gain.

1 TIMOTHY 6:6 NIV

Always There
in Time of Need

Grandma always made you feel she had been waiting
to see just you all day and now the day was complete.

MARCY DeMAREE

Those are red-letter days in our lives
when we meet people who thrill us like a fine poem...
people whose handshakes are brimful
of unspoken sympathy and whose sweet,
rich natures impart to our eager, impatient spirits
a wonderful restlessness which,
in its essence, is divine....
The solemn nothings that fill our everyday life
blossom suddenly into bright possibilities.
In a word, while such friends are near us
we feel that all is well.

HELEN KELLER

God will generously provide all you need.
Then you will always have everything you need
and plenty left over to share with others.

2 CORINTHIANS 9:8 NLT

Buttered rolls. Corn on the cob.
Watermelon from the garden. Iced sun tea.
These are the comfort foods of summer at Grandma's.

God's gifts make us truly wealthy.
His loving supply
never shall leave us wanting.

BECKY LAIRD

There will be days which are great and everything
goes as planned. There will be other days
when we aren't sure why we got out of bed.
Regardless of which kind of day it is,
we can be assured that God takes care
of our daily needs.

EMILIE BARNES

If you have a special need today, focus your full attention
on the goodness and greatness of your Father
rather than on the size of your need.
Your need is so small compared to
His ability to meet it.

It is not my business to think about myself.
My business is to think about God.
It is for God to think about me.

SIMONE WELL

Thank You God for Grandma,
She brings us all such joy,
And thank You for the love
she gives to every girl and boy.
Dear God, when I am bigger,
Help me, too, to see,
Life as a gift, to share in love,
And like my Grandma be.

I must simply be thankful, and I am,
for all the Lord has provided for me,
whether big or small in the eyes of someone else.

MABEL P. ADAMSON

You know both God and how He works. Steep your life in
God-reality, God-initiative, God-provisions.
Don't worry about missing out. You'll find all your
everyday human concerns will be met.

MATTHEW 6:30 THE MESSAGE

The oddities of shape that age has given me,
defeating exercise and diet, making me appear
hump-backed, pot-bellied, flabby-armed
when inside in reality I am slim and straight and,
bracing all my muscles, prove to be purpose-built
for carting grandchildren from place to place.
I am a breathing, ambulatory armchair;
the perfect place for cuddles.

PAM BROWN

Throughout the Bible, when God asked a man to
do something, methods, means, materials and
specific directions were always provided.
The man had one thing to do: obey.

ELISABETH ELLIOT

You do not really understand something
unless you can explain it to your grandmother.

A father to the fatherless,
a defender of widows,
is God in His holy dwelling.
God sets the lonely in families,
He leads forth the prisoners with singing....
When You went out before Your people, O God,...
the earth shook, the heavens poured down rain....
You gave abundant showers, O God;
You refreshed Your weary inheritance.
Your people settled in it,
and from Your bounty, O God,
You provided for the poor.

PSALM 68: 5-10 NIV

You can trust God right now
to supply all your needs for today.
And if your needs are more tomorrow,
His supply will be greater also.

Simplicity
Itself

Grandparent:
Something so simple a child can operate it.

Her eyes sparkle with warmth and love—years
and years of memories dance within their light.
She is my grandma and I feel safe when I can curl up
next to her, as we sip our cups of hot cocoa, laughing and
telling stories.

Grandmothers walk slowly and so rediscover
oil rainbows, fallen leaves, puddles
and worms in need of rescue.

JULIE B. JONES

A fiery sunset, tiny pansies by the wayside,
the sound of raindrops tapping on the roof—
what extraordinary delight we find
in the simple wonders of life!
With wide eyes and full hearts,
we may cherish what others often miss.

He shows those who are humble how to do right,
and He teaches them His ways.

PSALM 25:9 NCV

Not every day of our lives
is overflowing with joy and celebration.
But there are moments when our hearts nearly
burst within us for the sheer joy of being alive.
The first sight of our newborn babies,
the warmth of love in another's eyes,
the fresh scent of rain on a hot summer's eve—
moments like these renew in us
a heartfelt appreciation for life.

GWEN ELLIS

Enjoy the little things.
One day you may look back and realize...
they were the big things.

A devout life does bring wealth, but it's the
rich simplicity of being yourself before God.
Since we entered the world penniless
and will leave it penniless,
if we have bread on the table
and shoes on our feet, that's enough.

1 TIMOTHY 6:6 THE MESSAGE

Always stay connected to people
and seek out things that bring you joy.
Dream with abandon. Pray confidently.

BARBARA JOHNSON

Our lives are a mosaic of little things,
like putting a rose in a vase on the table.

INGRID TROBISCH

A little simplification would be the first step toward rational living, I think.

ELEANOR ROOSEVELT

Happy people...enjoy the fundamental, often very simple things of life.... They savor the moment, glad to be alive, enjoying their work, their families, the good things around them. They are adaptable; they can bend with the wind, adjust to the changes in their times, enjoy the contest of life.... Their eyes are turned outward; they are aware, compassionate. They have the capacity to love.

JANE CANFIELD

It isn't the great big pleasures that count the most; it's making a great deal out of the little ones.

JEAN WEBSTER

Year by year the complexities of this
spinning world grow more bewildering,
and so each year we need all the more
to seek peace and comfort
in the joyful simplicities.

So in everything, do to others
what you would have them do to you,
for this sums up the Law and the Prophets.

MATTHEW 7:12 NIV

A grandmother's love
is the blanket that wraps around you
on life's wintry days.

Abundant Blessings

You are a blessing sent from Heaven above,
a huggable reminder of God's unfailing love.

Tarry at the promise till God meets you there.
He always returns by way of His promises.

L. B. COWMAN

Having someone who understands you is home.
Having someone who loves you is belonging.
Having both is a blessing.

Grandma,
some of the greatest jewels in my life
are the words you have spoken to me of Jesus.

When You grant a blessing, O Lord,
it is an eternal blessing!

1 CHRONICLES 17:27 NLT

I wish I had a box, the biggest I could find,
I'd fill it right up to the brim with everything that's kind.
A box without a lock, of course, and never any key;
for everything inside that box would then be offered free.
Grateful words for joys received I'd freely give away.
Oh, let us open wide a box of praise for every day.

Let God's promises shine on your problems.

CORRIE TEN BOOM

When we start to count flowers,
we cease to count weeds;
When we start to count blessings,
we cease to count needs;
When we start to count laughter,
we cease to count tears;
When we start to count memories,
we cease to count years.

How great is Your goodness,
which You have stored up for those who fear You,
which You bestow in the sight of men
on those who take refuge in You.

PSALM 31:19 NIV

We should all have one person who knows
how to bless us despite the evidence,
Grandmother was that person to me.

PHYLLIS THEROUX

I will let God's peace infuse every part of today.
As the chaos swirls and life's demands
pull at me on all sides,
I will breathe in God's peace
that surpasses all understanding.
He has promised that He would set within me
a peace too deeply planted to be affected
by unexpected or exhausting demands.

Lift up your eyes. Your heavenly Father waits to bless you—in inconceivable ways to make your life what you never dreamed it could be.

ANNE ORTLUND

I may never be a millionaire
but I have something better than that.
I have my children, good friends,
a place to call home, and wonderful relatives.
These are so many of life's wonderful blessings!

God has not promised sun without rain,
joy without sorrow, peace without pain.
But God has promised strength for the day,
rest for the labor, light for the way,
grace for the trials, help from above,
unfailing sympathy, undying love.

ANNIE JOHNSON FLINT

Expressed affection is the best of all methods to use
when you want to light a glow in someone's heart
and to feel it in your own.

RUTH STAFFORD PEALE

Grandma, you share in my dreams
and spur on my adventures. Your stories inspire me
and your loving encouragement motivates me.
You're my very own cheering section.

You go before me and follow me.
You place your hand of blessing on my head.
Such knowledge is too wonderful for me,
too great for me to understand!

PSALM 139: 5-6 NLT

Spirit
of Truth

No love could be more steadfast,
No heart more kind and true,
No grandmother in the world could be
More precious, dear, than you.

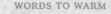
God who is goodness and truth is also beauty.
It is this innate human and divine longing,
found in the company of goodness and truth,
that is able to recognize and leap up at beauty
and rejoice and know that all is beautiful,
that there is not one speck of beauty under the sun
that does not mirror back the beauty of God.

ROBERTA BONDI

*Truth is always exciting.
Speak it, then.
Life is dull without it.*

PEARL S. BUCK

Jesus answered, "I am the way and the truth and the life.
No one comes to the Father except through Me."

JOHN 14:6 NIV

It is an extraordinary and beautiful thing that God,
in creation...works with the beauty of matter;
the reality of things; the discoveries of the senses,
all five of them;
so that we, in turn, may hear the grass growing;
see a face springing to life in love and laughter....
The offerings of creation...our glimpses of truth.

MADELIENE L'ENGLE

God sends children to enlarge our hearts
and to make us unselfish and
full of kindly sympathies and affections.

MARY HOWITT

Amid ancient lore the Word of God stands
unique and pre-eminent. Wonderful in its construction,
admirable in its adaptation, it contains truths that a child
may comprehend, and mysteries into which
angels desire to look.

FRANCES ELLEN WATKINS HARPER

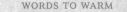
Stand firm then, with the belt of truth
buckled around your waist,
with the breastplate of righteousness in place,
and with your feet fitted with the readiness
that comes from the gospel of peace.

EPHESIANS 6:14-15 NIV

The wonder of our Lord is that
He is so accessible to us in the
common things of our lives:
the cup of water...breaking of the bread...
welcoming children into our arms...
fellowship over a meal...giving thanks.
A simple attitude of caring, listening,
and lovingly telling the truth.

NANCIE CARMICHAEL

Then Jesus said…, "If you abide
in My word, you are My disciples indeed.
And you shall know the truth,
and the truth shall make you free."

JOHN 8:31-32 NKJV

Open my eyes that I may see
Glimpses of truth Thou hast for me.
Place in my hands the wonderful key
That shall unclasp and set me free:
Silently now I wait for Thee,
Ready, my God, Thy will to see;
Open my eyes, illumine me,
Spirit divine!

CLARA H. SCOTT

The truth [is] that there is only one
terminal dignity—love. And the story of a love
is not important—what is important
is that one is capable of love.
It is perhaps the only glimpse
we are permitted of eternity.

HELEN HAYES

I am amazed by the sayings of Christ.
They seem truer than anything I have ever read.
And they certainly turn the world upside down.

KATHERINE BUTLER HATHAWAY

Beauty
of the Soul

You can take no credit for beauty at sixteen.
But if you are beautiful at sixty,
it will be your soul's own doing.

MARIE STOPES

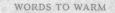
Isn't it a wonderful morning?
The world looks like something God
had just imagined for His own pleasure.

LUCY MAUD MONTGOMERY

If your baby is "beautiful and perfect,
never cries or fusses, sleeps on schedule
and burps on demand, an angel all the time"...
you're the grandma.

TERESA BLOOMINGDALE

Give unto the Lord the glory due to His name;
Worship the Lord in the beauty of holiness.

PSALM 29:2 NKJV

Something deep in all of us yearns for God's beauty,
and we can find it no matter where we are.

SUE MONK KIDD

· · · · · · · · · · · · · · · · · · · ·

Today a new sun rises for me;
everything lives, everything is animated,
everything seems to speak to me of my passion,
everything invites me to cherish it.

ANNE DE LENCLOS

*The heart always has room
for beautiful memories.*

Your beauty and love chase after me every day of my life.
I'm back home in the house of God for the rest of my life.

PSALM 23:6 THE MESSAGE

Let there be many windows in your soul,
That all the glory of the universe may beautify it.

ELLA WHEELER WILCOX

Beauty puts a face on God. When we gaze
at nature, at a loved one, at a work of art,
our soul immediately recognizes
and is drawn to the face of God.

MARGARET BROWNLEY

*May God give you eyes to see beauty only
the heart can understand*

As God's workmanship, we deserve to be treated,
and to treat ourselves, with affection and affirmation,
regardless of our appearance or performance.

MARY ANN MAYO

It is one of the most beautiful compensations of this life
that the more you give away to others, the more you get
to keep for yourself.

· · · · · · · · · · · · · · · · · · · ·

Therefore, as God's chosen people, holy and dearly
loved, clothe yourselves with compassion,
kindness, humility, gentleness and patience.

COLOSSIANS 3:12 NIV

You are God's created beauty
and the focus of His affection and delight.

JANET WEAVER SMITH

Life has loveliness to sell,
All beautiful and splendid things,
Blue waves whitened on a cliff,
Soaring fire that sways and sings...
Spend all you have for loveliness,
Buy it and never count the cost;
For one white singing hour of peace
Count many a year of strife well lost,
And for a breath of ecstasy
Give all you have been, or could be.

SARA TEASDALE

In all ranks of life the human heart
yearns for the beautiful,
and the beautiful things
that God makes
are His gift to all alike.

HARRIET BEECHER STOWE

My grandma has a look in her eyes like rubies
and a gentle, loving smile.

CARRIE DOUGLAS, AGE 9

One can get just as much exultation
in losing oneself in a little thing
as in a big thing.
It is nice to think how one can be
recklessly lost in a daisy!

ANNE MORROW LINDBERGH

Wisdom
to Share

What we need is not new light, but new sight;
not new paths, but new strength to walk in the old ones;
not new duties but new wisdom from on High
to fulfill those that are plain before us.

I am convinced beyond a shadow of any doubt
that the most valuable pursuit we can
embark upon is to know God.

KAY ARTHUR

*Teach us to number our days aright, that we
may gain a heart of wisdom.*

PSALM 90:12 NIV

At the end of your life you will never regret not having
passed one more test, not winning one more verdict,
or not closing one more deal. You will regret time not
spent with a husband, a friend, a child, or a parent.

BARBARA BUSH

The wise don't expect to find life worth living;
they make it that way.

Those gasps of astonishment, those shrieks of pleasure,
those sighs of delight, lost long ago when your children
grew wise and worldly, are suddenly given back to you
by your grandchildren.

PAM BROWN

We ought to be able to learn things secondhand.
There is not enough time for us to make
all the mistakes ourselves.

HARRIET HALL

It seems that we learn lessons when we least expect them
but always when we need them the most,
and the true "gift" in these lessons always lies
in the learning process itself.

CATHY LEE CROSBY

Would I wish to be young again?
No, for I've learned too much to wish to lose it.

PEARL S. BUCK

A wise gardener plants her seeds,
then has the good sense not to dig them up
every few days to see if a crop is on the way.
Likewise, we must be patient as God
brings the answers...in His own good time.

QUIN SHERRER

*In youth we learn;
in age we understand.*

MARIE VON EBNER-ESCHENBACH

Happy is the man who finds wisdom,
and the man who gains understanding;
for Wisdom's proceeds are better than the profits
of silver, and her gain than fine gold.

PROVERBS 3:13-14 NKJV